What people say about Nick James

"If you want your own online business, I'd say you'd want to learn from the guy that's been doing it for over a decade with OUTRAGEOUS Success! That would be my friend Nick James! And the best place to start is by reading this book!"

Bill Glazer
Best-Seller Author, Professional Speaker, Copywriter,
OutrageousCampaigns.com

"Nick's marketing methods are truly inspirational. You can't go far wrong if you stick to these principles and strategies, which is exactly why I believe you should read this book from cover to cover."

Clate Mask
Keap.com (formerly known as InfusionSoft.com)

"Nick James is a true inspiration to every business owner or budding new entrepreneur. It's no surprise that recently Nick won 'Internet Marketer Of The Year' as voted for by over 200 other business leaders and full-time marketers.

Matt Bacak,
MattBacak.com

"Nick gets straight to the point, providing the exact steps he takes in his own business, showing the way to make an additional six figures per year."

Laura Casselman
CEO, JVZoo.com

If you would like to share your thoughts and feedback about this book or any of our other products and services, we invite you to leave your own comments online at:
www.MyCustomerComments.com

First Printing: 2021

Copyright © 2021 by Nick James
All rights reserved.

Printed in the United Kingdom.

All rights reserved. This book or any of its parts may not be reproduced or used in any manner whatsoever without the express written permission of the author and publisher. However, brief quotations in a book review or scholarly journal are permitted.

Authors and their publications mentioned in this work and bibliography have their copyright protection. All brand and product names used in this book are trademarks, registered trademarks, or trade names and belong to the respective owners.

The author is unassociated with any product or vendor in this book.

The Handy Book Of Great Ideas For Information Publishers

101 Tips, Insights, Ideas, Suggestions, Methods, Hacks, Templates, Shortcuts, Resources, and Lists

Nick James

Contents

Acknowledgements ix
About the Author xi
Introduction 1
Stage One Decisions: Key Insights For Planning Out Your Product, So It Sells 5
   1. Determine Who You're Targeting 5
   2. Find Out What People Want 6
   3. Four Ways To Find Out What Your Market Is Buying 6
   4. Profiling Your Target Market 7
   5. Two Ways To Test Your Ideas Fast 8
   6. Decide The Best Format 8
   7. Plan Your Extras 9
   8. Do Your Research 9
   9. Read Your Prospect's Reviews 10
   10. Survey Your Audience 10
   11. Three Ways To Organize Your Outline 10
   12. An Example Outline Template 11
   13. Determine Modules 12
   14. Planning Delivery 12
   15. Decide: DIY Or Outsource? 13
   16. Three Tips For Finding A Great Freelancer 13
   17. Three Tips for DIY Product Creation 14
   18. Define Your Product Goals 14
Stage Two Developments: Key Insights For Preparing Your Info Product, So It Satisfies. 15
   19. Develop an Appealing Title 15
   20. Choosing A Video Style 16
   21. 5 Pieces Of Equipment Needed To Create A Video-Based Product. 16
   22. Get A Professional Voice-Over Artist 17
   23. Three Tips For Creating Awesome Videos 17
   24. Tools Needed For Creating Text-Based Info Products 18
   25. Three Tips For Creating Awesome Lessons 18
   26. Identify Your USP 19
   27. Start With Your Credentials 19
   28. Three Tips For Creating A Fabulous Introduction 20
   29. Get Attention With This Storytelling Opener Template 21
   30. Craft Catchy Module Titles 22
   31. How To Close Each Module 22

32. Two Templates For Building Anticipation 23
33. How To Open A New Module 23
34. Using Curiosity To Keep People Engaged 24
35. Three Tips For Creating A Better Product 25
36. 13 Tools To Include With Your Product 25
37. How To Decide Which Tools To Include 26
38. Three Tips For Creating Graphics 27
39. Selling Within Your Info Product 27
40. Ten Places To Promote Your Backend Offer 28
41. Give Away Free Tools And Training 29
42. Craft A Call To Action (CTA) 29
43. 16 Types Of Profitable Backend Offers 29
44. Three Tips For Selling Affiliate Offers 30
45. Use A Conversational Tone 31
46. Five Ways To Engage Viewers 31
47. Inject Humor 32
48. Share Fresh, New Tips 32
49. Present Your Product In A Unique Way 33
50. Offer Examples 33
51. Two Tips For Being A Better Teacher 34
52. Help Non-Linear Thinkers 34
53. Use Graphical Representations 35
54. Three Ways To Add Value To Your Product 35
55. Create A High-Value Bonus Package 35
56. How To Create A Successful Private Group 37
57. Three Ways To Engage Customers In Your Group 37
58. Integrate Your Branding 38
59. A Secret For Creating A Great Product 38
60. Staying On Track 38

Stage Three Details: Key Insights For Polishing Your Product, So That It Shines 41
61. The #1 Bonus Mistake To Avoid 41
62. How To Price Your Product 42
63. Three Tips For Editing A Video-Based Product 43
64. Three Tips For Editing A Text-Based Product 43
65. The #1 Proofing Tip 44
66. Polish Your Product 44
67. Check Your Facts 45
68. Get Beta Readers 45
69. Test Your Titles 45
70. Set Up An Autoresponder 46
71. 5 Things To Include In Your Customer Email 47
72. Template For An Effective First Email 47

73. Load Your Autoresponder 48
74. Get Customer Feedback..49
75. Use A Soft Sell 50
76. Splinter Your Info Product...50
77. Exude Professionalism 50
78. Outsource The Sales Letter..51
79. DOs And DON'Ts For Convincing Prospects To Become Buyers ...52
80. Sell Your Videos Here..53
81. Setting Up Your Own Platform..53
82. Determining Delivery Details...54
83. A Helpful Idea For Reducing Refunds 55
84. Boosting Your Product's Credibility...55
85. The #1 High-Value Bonus Your Customers Will Love......................55
86. Assigning Homework..56
87. Create A Quick Start Guide 56
88. Write A "Stick" Letter..56
89. Offer Unannounced Bonuses 57
90. Gather Testimonials..57
91. Collect Together Case Studies...58
92. Start Planning Spin-Off Products 58
93. 11 Places To Cross-Promote Your Product...59
94. Check The Product Orientation 59
95. 4 Ways To Accelerate Product Creation 60
96. Three Content Creation Mistakes To Avoid......................................60
97. Three Questions To Ask Before You Launch Your Product..............61
98. Planning Your Sales Funnel 62
99. Four Characteristics Every Free Offer Ought To Possess 63
100. Check, Check, Double-Check 63
101. Testing Your Sales Process..64
Conclusion 65
Recommended Resources...67

Acknowledgements

As you are about to discover, this book is a little different from anything else we've published in the past. Therefore, instead of mentioning the names of various authors, speakers and thought leaders who have previously inspired me on my own entrepreneurial journey, I would like to lead the acknowledgments in this book by recognising the importance of you.

Our customer.

Because, without you and without the insights my wife and I have gained from listening to you, answering your emails, and responding to your support tickets over the years, I would not have been able to write this book.

We are ever grateful to you.

I also want to personally thank my wife and business partner Kate and our dedicated team of freelancers who help us to implement hundreds of ideas each year, from creating new marketing materials, to tracking campaigns, split testing, and studying our results to ultimately find out what works.

Of course, what works is what I've written about extensively within the pages of this very book, and it's my pleasure to be able to share these 101 tips, insights, ideas, suggestions, methods, hacks, templates, shortcuts, resources and lists with you.

It is our hope that by implementing what you learn and remaining dedicated to your Information Publishing business, that we may, in the future, be able to feature your accomplishments as a case study, in a forthcoming book called *The Six Figure Earners*.

Each case study in this new book will feature customers that have generated in excess of $100k from creating and selling products online.

All our customers are welcome to be included in the new book.

To be considered for the first edition, please be sure to keep our support team up-to-date with your business progress, either via email at admin@nickjamesadmin.com or by raising a new support ticket using any of the dedicated support desks available within any of our private membership areas.

I look forward to hearing your thoughts and feedback about the content of this book and of course about your continued business success over the months and years to come.

Kindest,

Nick James

About the Author

Nick James has built 3 separate million dollar a year internet businesses since his entrepreneurial journey began in 2001.

Nick is a true example of a self-made success and it's his own personal experience that makes him understanding and approachable on all business levels, working with enthusiastic entrepreneurs at varying stages of their journey into business.

Business coach, mentor, software developer, internet marketing expert – Nick James won *'Internet Marketer Of The Year'* 2016-2017 and won *'Outrageous Marketer Of The Year'* in 2020.

Websites:

> www.Nick-James.com
> www.SixFiguresAYear.com
> www.SeriousAboutSixFigures.com

Introduction

Picture this... it's New Year's Eve, and among all the celebrations that are taking place around the world to welcome in the new year, together with all the music, dancing, and fireworks, there's also a continuous 'pinging sound' coming from your cell phone lying next to you, a sound not caused by friends and family sending you well-wishes for the new year ahead, but instead, each 'ping' being yet another notification to let you know that someone else has just purchased your latest info product online. You have created a product, set it up for sale, and so many people are now buying it, you couldn't stop the sales from coming in (even if you wanted to).

Wouldn't those continued sales, and the reassurance that people had a desire to learn new skills from you, put you in the right frame of mind for the New Year ahead?

To know that your fully automated Info Publishing Business was working hard for you while you continued to celebrate?

Well, that's exactly what happened to us just over a year ago now, just as my wife Kate and I released our book *Six Figures A Year In Info Publishing* during the Christmas and New Year holidays.

In fact, as I write this, I have just fired up my laptop and checked our sales history during that exact week between Christmas Day and New Year's Day. My phone pinged a total of 2,960 times during that period, telling me about a new book sale, and it has continued to 'ping' pretty much every single day since then, turning that book into a best seller, whereby we have now shipped copies to customers living in all seven continents of the world.

Why am I telling you this?

Well, not only does it perfectly set the scene for how fantastic your life can be running a successful Info Publishing business, but it also explains how this very book has come about.

While it's not a sequel, this book would never have been written without first having published *Six Figures A Year In Info Publishing*. That's because each of the ideas that have been included in this book started off life as questions from customers who read my original book and got in touch with us. (*Perhaps you even helped to write this book – by asking a question. If so, thank you*). The answers to those questions have now formed the basis of this book.

We have now reformatted our original responses and compiled everything together into this, "The Handy Book Of Great Ideas For Information Publishers." It is packed full of 101 tips, insights, ideas, suggestions, methods, hacks, templates, shortcuts, resources, and lists that will help you create amazing products that your audience will love.

Why will they love your products?

Because you're going to learn the best practices for creating information products that truly help your audience.

You'll learn these tips and ideas across the three different stages of creating a new info product:

- Stage 1: ***Decisions.*** Here you'll get key insights for planning out your product, so it sells like gangbusters.

- Stage 2: ***Developments***. Here you'll get key insights for preparing your product, so it's virtually guaranteed to satisfy even the most demanding of customers.

- Stage 3: ***Details***. Here you'll get key insights for polishing your info product, so it truly shines and will become something you are extremely proud to offer for sale.

Whether you consider yourself to be a beginner or an experienced Information Publisher, if you have read my original book (or not), if you sell information products online or if you would like to... then you are in for a real treat.

> **Hot Tip:** If you don't have a copy of my first book, Six Figures A Year In Info Publishing, while stocks last, you can request a free copy (if you agree to pay just a small contribution towards the S&H) by visiting the following website: www.SixFiguresAYear.com

With that said, without further ado, let's get started.

1

Stage One Decisions:
Key Insights For Planning Out Your Product, So It Sells

One of the keys to creating a great info product is to spend ample time planning it. Below you'll find some of the key decisions you need to make, along with tips for navigating the planning stage successfully.

1. Determine Who You're Targeting

Have you selected a niche market (aka "target audience") yet? If not, then you need to look for a market with these characteristics:

- **Profitable**. Not only should your market be big enough to be profitable for you, but it also needs to be a market that is willing, able, and eager to spend money to get the results they want.

- **Evergreen**. Don't jump on fad markets. Stick to markets that will be around for the long term. You want to build a business that has both a steady supply of new customers, as well as returning ones.

- **Easily Reachable**. In other words, you should be able to reach the market online using both free and paid advertising.

How do you determine if a market is profitable? Run a search for your niche keywords (such as "dog training") both in Google and marketplaces such as Amazon.com, and look for plenty of products being sold and plenty of marketers (competition) doing the selling.

Next...

2. Find Out What People Want

Once you have a niche, then you need to pick a topic for your info product. Here again, you'll do market research in order to determine what people in your niche want. Here are two ways to figure this out:

1. **Survey your audience.** Don't use this method in isolation, as what people SAY they want can be different than their behavior (i.e., what they actually buy).

2. **Find out what people are already buying in your market.** Then seek to create something that's better than the current offerings.

Which brings us to the next tip...

3. Four Ways To Find Out What Your Market Is Buying

A good way to find out what people want is to determine what they're already buying. Here's how:

- **Search marketplaces.** This includes Amazon.com, ClickBank.com, and JVZoo.com. Look at the bestselling products and other info-products in your niche.

- **Search Google for your keywords**. You can also search for the word "course," "eBook," or "How To" alongside your keywords (e.g., dog training course). See what your top competitors are selling.

- **Browse the Google-sponsored listings when you do the above search**. If a marketer invests money to advertise an eBook (or other information product), that's a sign the product is selling.

- **Check Udemy for your keywords**. This site only sells video courses, so it will give you a good feel for your market.

In all cases, check out bestselling info products from other vendors as well as those with a lot of competition (e.g., several info products on the same topic). These both indicate a profitable market.

4. Profiling Your Target Market

In order to create a great info product for your market, you need to understand who you're selling to. That's why you'll want to learn as much as you can about this market. Check out these tips:

- **Listen to them online**. Read the forum, group, and blog discussions in this niche. Be sure to read product reviews too on Amazon.com and elsewhere to get a feel for the market.

- **Join the market.** Do what they do. For example, if you're selling to bodybuilders, then go to a bodybuilding gym three times per week.

- **Survey them**. Learn about their demographic information (age, gender, location, etc.) as well as what they want, their challenges in the market, and what they'd like to see in a new product.

- **Research them**. Search Google for your niche market alongside the word "demographics" (e.g., dog owner demographics). Be sure to do this research using reputable sources, such as Pew research or research conducted through accredited universities.

Next...

5. Two Ways To Test Your Ideas Fast

You have an idea for an Info Product – but will it fly? Use these two methods to find out:

1. **Create a "lite" version of the product**. This could be 5-10 lessons or even a small report. If people purchase this version of the product, then it's likely they'll purchase a more comprehensive product on the same topic.

2. **Take part in a "lite" promotion for a competitor**. Find a product similar to the one you intend to create and do a small promotion as an affiliate. This will earn you some quick commissions while allowing you to gauge interest.

Now the next decision...

6. Decide The Best Format

Once you have a niche and topic for your info product, then you need to decide how you'll deliver the information. Your main options include:

- Text-based product delivered all at once.
- Multipart eCourse delivered over time by email or other means.
- Video-based product delivered all at once.
- Multipart video product delivered over time.
- Audio product delivered all at once.
- Multipart audio product delivered over time.

Note: In most cases, you'll want to choose either the video course or the text-based product. You can offer the audio version as a bonus, but you may not necessarily want to offer JUST audio content.

Decide on a format based on the content of the product. If the viewers need to hear something (like a foreign language), then choose video. If they need to see you demonstrate something (like how to change a tire), then choose video there too.

Next...

7. Plan Your Extras

As you begin the initial planning for your info product, you'll want to start thinking about what types of bonuses or accessories to include with it.

For example, if you have a debt-management info product, then you might include budgeting worksheets.

As another example: if you're selling a dieting info product, then you might offer a meal-planning app as a bonus.

In short, your planning should include what sort of tools, resources, and extra information you can offer to help your customers implement the information in the product.

8. Do Your Research

In order to create your outline as well as the actual product itself, you'll want to research the topic so that you don't miss sharing any important pieces of information. This is applicable even if you know the information.

For example, if you're teaching people how to do Facebook marketing, then run those search words in Google to find out what sort of information others are sharing on this topic. Be sure you only pay attention to information from experts in your niche, scholarly sources, and other reputable sources.

9. Read Your Prospect's Reviews

One way to get a feel as to what your prospects really want is to read their reviews on similar products on sites like Amazon.com. Note these two things:

- **Customers will tell you what they like about products.** These are product strengths, and you'll want to have similar strengths in your own products.

- **Customers will tell you what they don't like about products.** These are product flaws/weaknesses, and your goal is to improve upon them.

End result: your product will be similar to what's selling well, but your product will be better than everything else out there.

10. Survey Your Audience

So, what else should you include in your product? Here's an idea: ask your audience. You can ask informally on Facebook, your blog, or via your newsletter. Or you can distribute a survey (using SurveyMonkey.com) to find out what features and topics your audience really wants in a new product.

This is a great way to plan out your "talking points".

11. Three Ways To Organize Your Outline

Once you've done your research to figure out what to include in your product, then you need to create your outline. How you organize it depends on what you're teaching. Here are three ideas:

- **Chronologically** (**step 1, step 2, etc.**). Good for how-to information.

- **Beginner to advanced.** Here the information doesn't necessarily need to be applied in a certain order, but some of the information is easier to understand than other parts.

- **Fast results to those that take longer.** For example, placing a paid ad on Facebook can yield fast results (traffic can flow in a matter of an hour or so), while optimizing a site for a search engine takes longer.

Which brings us to the next point...

12. An Example Outline Template

Many product creators share step-by-step information. Here's an example of what the outline may look like:

A. **Introduction** – tell your audience what they'll learn and build anticipation for the benefits they'll receive.

B. **Step 1**

Explanation of this step.
Tips and examples.
Take action tools or assignment(s).

C. **Step 2**

Explanation of this step.
Tips and examples.
Take action tools or assignment(s).

D. **Step 3**

Explanation of this step.

Tips and examples.
Take action tools or assignment(s).

E. Conclusion

Review of what the audience learned.
Call to action.

13. Determine Modules

If all of your steps are about the same size (in terms of the time it takes to explain them), then you can simply break your content up with each step being a separate module.

However, if some steps take longer to explain, then you may want to break up these steps into multiple smaller steps. That way, each lesson or module for the steps is shorter, easier to consume, and easier to implement (because the user isn't overwhelmed).

14. Planning Delivery

Another issue you need to consider is whether you intend to deliver the product all at once or break it up and deliver it via email (or a membership site "drip") over time.

Delivering it all at once provides instant gratification and lets users go at their own pace. This can boost customer satisfaction (depending on the topic).

Delivering it over time via email means you get a chance to promote something via email that your students are sure to see. In addition, users won't get as overwhelmed if a complex process is delivered over time or if there is a LOT of information to share.

Next…

15. Decide: DIY Or Outsource?

Ask yourself these questions to help you decide whether to create your new product yourself or outsource it:

- **Do you have the skills to create it yourself?** Would a freelancer be able to do a better job?

- **Do you have the time to create it yourself?** What could you be doing instead of creating the product?

- **How much would it cost you to do it yourself?** Multiply the number of hours it would take you to do it by your per hour worth, (e.g., if your time is worth $100 an hour, and the new product would take you 40 hours, then it costs you $4000 to do it yourself).

- **Can a freelancer do it at less cost than your above calculation?**

- **Do you have the cash on hand to outsource it?** If not, how could you raise the money to outsource it?

Next...

16. Three Tips For Finding A Great Freelancer

If you decide to outsource, then you'll want to check out these three tips for finding and hiring a great freelancer:

- **Look in multiple places.** Search Google, ask friends for recommendations, and post projects on freelancing sites such as upwork.com.

- **Do your due diligence.** Research each potential freelancer thoroughly by searching for their name in Google, checking their references, reviewing their portfolio, and browsing their feedback ratings on freelancing sites.

- **Test freelancers.** Hire multiple freelancers for small projects and then see who provides the best quality work and service.

Planning on doing it yourself? Check out this next tip...

17. Three Tips for DIY Product Creation

Create a better product by following these three do-it-yourself tips:

- **Create a thorough outline first.** If the outline is detailed, then writing the content for your product will be a breeze.

- **Write first, edit later.** This tends to create a better end product, plus it also helps you avoid getting "stuck" on certain parts.

- **Cut out distractions.** Ask household members not to interrupt you when you're working, and use an app like GetColdTurkey.com if you need to eliminate online distractions.

Here's another good tip...

18. Define Your Product Goals

Don't even think about writing a single word of your product's content until you define your product goals and outcomes.

Specifically:

- What do you want your readers to LEARN in each lesson?
- What do you want your readers to DO in each lesson?

Now the next step...

2

Stage Two Developments:
Key Insights For Preparing Your Info Product, So It Satisfies.

Now it's time to start developing your product.

So, let us check out these additional ideas...

19. Develop an Appealing Title

Many of your prospects are going to form their initial impression of your product and even decide whether they want to buy it based on the title. That's why you'll want to spend time brainstorming titles. Follow these tips:

- **Use a benefit-driven title.** In other words, tell people what they're going to learn or achieve. E.G., "How To Have An Amazing First Year Of Homeschooling" or "How To Start an Organic Garden (Even If You Don't Have A Green Thumb)."

- **Offer a quicker, easier, or better solution.** E.G., "Walk More, Weigh Less: The Guide To Walking Off The Pounds" or "Marathon Training For Busy People."

Next...

20. Choosing A Video Style

If you're creating a video-based product, then choose a video style that will help you convey the information in the best way possible. Your main options include:

- **Talking head video**. Where you (or someone else) look directly at the camera and share the information.

- **Slide-presentation.** Video with text and graphics, which may or may not include voice-over narration.

- **Demo video.** Which is where you show viewers how to do something.

- **Animated video.** Which is where you can show demos or illustrate the video using animated figures. (This requires more skill than the above options, but it can be entertaining if done right.)

For example, if your video teaches people how to eat well to lose weight, then a talking head video or slide presentation would work well. If your video shows people how to perform an exercise, then a demo video or animated video would be better options.

21. 5 Pieces Of Equipment Needed To Create A Video-Based Product

If you're creating a video-based product, then you'll need one or more of the following pieces of equipment (depending on the type of video you're creating):

- **A good mic.** The company Audio Technica has several good microphones. The AT2020 USB mic has been particularly popular with product creators in the past.

- **A good camera.** Check your phone cameras and other cameras first, as many of them shoot quality, high-definition videos.

- **A simple backdrop.** If you're doing talking head videos or even demos, be sure your backdrop is clean and simple.

- **Slide presentation software.** You can use popular software such as PowerPoint or even online software like the one found at Prezi.com.

- **Screen-recording software and video editing.** Camtasia is a popular choice, which you can find at https://www.techsmith.com/video-editor.html.

Next…

22. Get A Professional Voice-Over Artist

Don't have the speaking voice to create a professional-sounding video? No problem, because you can hire a professional voice-over artist. Here's the best place to find plenty of talent: www.voices.com.

23. Three Tips For Creating Awesome Videos

Keep these tips in mind if you're creating video content:

- **Use professional graphics and layouts**. Don't skimp on this, otherwise your entire video will look like the work of an amateur. (If needed, hire a professional designer to create your graphics).

- **Don't do it all in one take.** Instead, use smaller takes (just a minute or two long) and then piece them together during the editing process to create your video.

- **Keep the tempo upbeat.** This includes both the audio and visuals. Check popular tutorials on YouTube to get a feel for how fast the audio and visuals change.

Next...

24. Tools Needed For Creating Text-Based Info Products

If you're creating a text-based info product, then you'll need the following tools:

- **A word processor.** Check your device for an existing word processor (such as Microsoft Word). You can also try the open-source alternative at OpenOffice.org.

- **A PDF converter.** Again, check your Word Processor software to see if you have a solution that can convert text documents to PDF. If not, try a program like PDFForge.org.

- **Graphics**. If you're creating graphics for your content, try a tool like Canva.com, Pixlr.com, or Gimp.org.

Next...

25. Three Tips For Creating Awesome Lessons

If you're creating a text-based info product, then check out these tips for keeping people engaged and reading:

- **Share something really good (one of your best tips) right in the first minute.** This will keep people engaged and eager to keep reading.

- **Organize your content with subheadings.** And be sure the subheadings include benefits or attention-getting information, which will draw skimmers back into the content.

- **Format for easy readability**. This includes short words, short sentences, and short paragraphs. Ensure there is plenty of white space, so the content is easy on the eyes.

Here's another tip...

26. Identify Your USP

Before you begin crafting your info product, it's a good idea to define your unique selling proposition. This is the reason why people should buy your product instead of, or in addition to, those of your competition. How are you uniquely qualified to help them? Once you know this information, you can reflect it on the sales page, your website, and within the content.

Here are examples of a USP:

- You have unique credentials to teach the content.

- You teach the content in a unique way (e.g., you share a proprietary "system" or "formula").

- You offer a unique or strong guarantee.

- You offer customer service that's different from your competitors (e.g., 24/7 service).

- Your info product has a claim to fame of being first in some category (e.g., the first product of its type to be created for work at home moms, or the first kind to be video-based).

And another tip...

27. Start With Your Credentials

No matter what sort of info product you've created, you should open by telling readers or viewers why they should listen to you. To determine what to share with your audience, ask yourself these questions:

- Do you have any sort of related degree or certifications?
- What related job experience do you have?
- Do you have any unpaid experience?
- Have you produced results for yourself?
- Have you produced results for others?
- Have you won any awards or accolades in the field?

Don't dwell on this in your content (as no one bought it to learn about you), but do take a moment to share relevant information.

NOTE: It isn't necessary to do this in the product content itself. To establish your credibility, you can share this background information about yourself in the sales letter or in free content that you give away.

The point of this is not to brag about yourself or your accomplishments, but rather to demonstrate to your audience that you are well qualified to help them get the results they desire.

They need to believe that you can help them.

28. Three Tips For Creating A Fabulous Introduction

The introduction to your product is really important because it's going to set the tone for the entire product. And if your introduction is boring or doesn't motivate people, then they simply won't make it through the rest of the content.

> *Sidebar: Nobody wins if your customers don't consume your information, take action and see results. They don't get the help they need. And you don't get to make a difference in the life of the customer, satisfy the customer, and secure future business from the customer.*

That's why you'll want to follow these three tips for creating an attention-getting introduction:

- **Start with a great opening line/paragraph.** You want to grab (and hold) your audience's attention right from the first few words.

- **Tell people the benefits they'll receive.** In other words, build anticipation for what's coming and get the audience excited about the benefits.

- **Arouse curiosity about what they'll learn.** This is a good way to keep people engaged and reading. E.G., "You'll discover a simple hack for saving hundreds of dollars on your next Disney vacation."

Next...

29. Get Attention With This Storytelling Opener Template

One way to capture your audience's attention right from the get-go is to tell a story. Here's an example template:

I couldn't believe it – I [had some terrible result, e.g., "the scale showed I had gained weight, and I was supposed to be on a diet"].

Tell you what, I felt absolutely [insert how you felt]. I thought [I'd never get results]. I was ready to give up.

And then something wonderful happened…

I discovered [brief description of what was discovered that gave better results]. Suddenly [explain how you got better results]. And most amazing of all, [explain another way that you got great results].

How did I do it?

Simple: [give an overview of the "discovery"].

And that's what this [lesson/module] is about, where you too will discover how to [get some great result].

30. Craft Catchy Module Titles

Just as people make a buying decision based on the title of your product, they're also going to make watching/reading decisions based on the titles of your modules/chapters. That's why you'll want to create benefit-driven, attention-grabbing module titles.

For example:

- *The [#] Smartest Things You Can Do To [Get a Result]*
  Example: The 10 Smartest Things You Can Do To Improve Your Credit Rating

- *[Number] Surprising Reasons [Why You Get Or Do Not Get a Result]*
  Example: Six Surprising Reasons Why You Are Dieting And Exercising Without Losing Weight

- *A Simple [Number] Step Formula for [Getting a Specific Result]*
  Example: A Simple Five-Step Formula For Starting A Successful Podcast

NOTE: The above three title templates were taken from a free PDF called "25 Content Title Templates That Get Attention," which you can download at: www.Nick-James.com/title-templates

31. How To Close Each Module

The conclusion for each module should include these pieces:

- A summary of what the student just learned.

- A take-action tool, such as a worksheet or assignment.

- An exciting look at what's coming up in the next module (to build anticipation and keep users engaged).

Which brings us to the next point...

32. Two Templates For Building Anticipation

Check out these two sample templates for building anticipation:

Example 1:

> *Don't go anywhere! That's because in the next lesson you're going to learn a surprisingly simple way to [get some benefit/result]. Click here to keep reading.*

Example 2:

> *You're going to love what's coming up in Module [#]! You'll find out how to [get some good result], plus you'll also discover an easy hack for [getting a benefit]. Click here to watch the next video.*

33. How To Open A New Module

Keep in mind that not everyone is going to watch all your modules back-to-back. As such, each new module should include the following pieces:

- **Recap of the previous module.** This reminds viewers of the previous module if it's been a while since they read/watched it. This recap should also entice students to consume the previous module if they haven't already done so.

- **Overview of what's coming in the current module.** As always, you want to build anticipation to keep people reading/viewing. This is all about helping people make progress.

For example:

> *"Inside this lesson, you'll find out the one thing that you should*

NEVER do when training for your first marathon – most runners make this mistake and suffer unnecessarily because of it."
Next...

34. Using Curiosity To Keep People Engaged

You want your readers or viewers to consume everything you have created. And one good way to do that is by arousing curiosity about what's coming up later in the product.

For example:

"In just a minute, you'll discover which 'healthy' food will actually sabotage your dieting progress – you probably ate this food today! But first, check out these three tips for raising your metabolism."

This is a good time to bring up this point...

Everything about your product should help facilitate movement toward the desired outcome.

Why do you want readers to get excited about buying your product? Why do you want them to eagerly look forward to each module? Why do you want them to read the opening, the middle, and the close? Why do you want them to complete assignments, take steps and read/view the next lesson?

All of it should work towards helping them get the result they desire.

All. Of. It.

We strategically do all of these things because it's to the advantage of our customers that we do them. It's in their best interests. It keeps them moving toward the end and the outcome they are working towards.

And ... that helps us too. It increases satisfaction and reduces refunds. It gets the customer coming back for more and bringing others with them through referrals.

Everybody. Wins.

35. Three Tips For Creating A Better Product

You can increase customer satisfaction by following these tips for creating a better product:

- **Be sure your product solves a specific problem.** Don't try to be all things to all people in your niche. Pick a very specific niche, and solve a problem for them.

- **Explain why your process works.** Don't just tell people what to do – tell them WHY they should complete the process in this particular way. Giving people the 'why' helps eliminate analysis paralysis.

- **Connect with viewers/readers on an emotional level.** Share a relevant, personal story. This will help bond students to you, build trust, and help them relate to you because there are overlaps in your stories, experiences, values, and goals.

Next...

36. 13 Tools To Include With Your Product

One way to create satisfied customers is to provide them with the tools they need to implement the information they learned in the product. Here are tools you can offer:

- Checklists
- Worksheets
- Cheat sheets
- Templates
- Swipes
- Planners/calendars

- Gear lists
- Glossary of terms
- Mind maps
- Process maps
- Video demos
- Access to a membership site
- Access to a live or replayed webinar
- Additional resources to get more information, including eBooks/reports, videos, and audios

Which brings us to the next point...

37. How To Decide Which Tools To Include

Here are three questions to ask yourself which will help you determine what sorts of tools to include in your overall product package:

- What is the overall goal for the product? That is, what should students accomplish?

- What steps should my students take at the end of each lesson?

- What type of tool would best help students take the needed action steps?

For example, let's suppose you're teaching people how to complete a marathon. The overall goal is to teach people how to properly train for the race. Each lesson gives the students information on different aspects of that training (workouts, nutrition, recovery, gear, motivation, etc.).

Your tools might include:

- *A set of workouts to complete during the training (speed, long run, recovery, etc.).*

- *A multi-week training schedule with a breakdown of what type of workout to complete and paces to hit.*

- *A race-day checklist that includes all of the steps/items that make for a successful outcome.*

Here's the next tip...

38. Three Tips For Creating Graphics

To make a great impression with your product, you need great graphics. Check out these ideas:

- **Use Canva.com.** This is a tool that makes it relatively easy for beginners to create beautiful graphics.

- **Hire someone.** For simple graphics, you can try Fiverr.com. For something more complex, hire a pro from Upwork.com, or search for graphic designers using Google.

- **Purchase graphics.** You can purchase simple graphics on stock photo sites such as istockphoto.com and depositphoto.com.

Next...

39. Selling Within Your Info Product

Don't even think about creating your product until you've determined what you're going to sell on the backend. That way, your content can be crafted to naturally lead to another offer you're promoting.

> *TIP: Sell something that solves another part of your customer's problem or helps them solve the current problem faster and easier. For example, if you're selling a product on how to write a sales letter, then sell a package of templates and swipes to help them create sales letters faster and easier.*

40. Ten Places To Promote Your Backend Offer

One of the keys to a profitable product is to promote a related, in-demand backend offer. Here are 10 places to promote it:

- At the beginning of your product
- At the end of the product
- At the end of a lesson
- Embedded within the content itself
- Within a 'Recommended Resources' section
- Inside the emails that deliver the lessons/modules
- Inside the membership site where students download content
- On the download page
- Within general follow-up emails sent to students
- In a private group or forum

Again, let's be clear about the goal here: Mutual benefit.

These related *'backend'* offers give additional help to the existing customer (usually by making the process faster or easier) and create additional sales opportunities for you.

You. Both. Benefit.

That said, these backend offers should be OPTIONAL. That is, when someone buys your info product, it should deliver on what was promised to them in the sales process. They shouldn't have to make any additional purchase to implement what you teach (*unless it was disclosed in the sales process*).

The truth is this: if you deliver what you promise in your product AND offer something related to enhance the product even further, many people will gladly pay for the extra resource. But if you don't deliver what you promise, they won't likely do business with you again.

Here's the next tip...

41. Give Away Free Tools And Training

Another option for 'selling within your product's content' is to give away free content that leads to another related offer.

Example: If you look back at this very guide, you'll see that I gave you two additional resources so far: 25 Content Title Templates That Get Results and The Content Creation Worksheet. Both of these PDFs are high value and useful in and of themselves. However, the webpage where you download them also contains an advertisement for a complete package of content creation cheat sheets with a special $100 off coupon.

Which brings us to the next point...

42. Craft A Call To Action (CTA)

Whenever you're promoting your backend offer, you'll need to create a CTA (call to action) which is where you specifically tell people what you want them to do next. Ideally, you should give them a reason to take action right away.

For example: "There is no need for you to rack your brain trying to come up with the perfect lesson title when you can simply fill in the blanks of these proven templates. Just like that, you've got a winning title. Take this shortcut by downloading your copy now and use the time you saved for other things."

43. 16 Types Of Profitable Backend Offers

What sort of products can you sell on the backend to those who purchase your new info product? Check out these ideas:

- Access to membership sites
- Additional courses on related topics
- eBooks/reports
- Coaching/consulting
- Videos (including webinar replays)

- Audios
- Apps/software/plugins
- Templates
- Swipes
- Planners/calendars
- Cheat sheets
- Mind maps
- Process maps
- Physical products
- Affiliate offers
- Content licensing

Here's an example...

> *If you sell any kind of info product that requires your customer to create their own content, then offering PLR (private label rights) licensing to existing content is a good idea. PLR gives your customer a quick and easy shortcut to creating the content they need while providing you an opportunity to earn a backend sale. Obviously, each customer might be creating content in various niches, so you could recommend several different websites that sell PLR content in multiple major niches.*

That's important to note: your backend offer doesn't even have to be YOUR offer...

44. Three Tips For Selling Affiliate Offers

If you promote affiliate offers (you earn a commission referring customers to other vendors) on the backend of your product, then you'll want to check out these tips:

- **Review and use all products.** Don't promote unless you've personally reviewed the product.

- **Redirect affiliate links through your own website.** That way, if you change your mind about an affiliate offer OR if the affiliate link goes dead, you can quickly and easily change the link to a different offer.

- **Replace affiliate offers with your own offers where applicable.** For example, if you're selling a pack of templates with an affiliate link, then work on creating your own template pack to sell to your customers. Better to make 100% of every sale than 50%.

Next…

45. Use A Conversational Tone

Whether you're creating a text-based info product or writing the script for a video course, be sure to use a friendly, conversational tone. Indeed, imagine that you're sharing this information with a friend, and write it as you would speak to that friend.

In short, avoid stiff "textbook style" and use a friendly tone instead to keep users engaged.

Which brings us to the next point…

46. Five Ways To Engage Viewers

In order to create a successful product, you need to keep students engaged and reading/viewing throughout the whole thing, as we've mentioned before. Here are five ways to engage your audience:

- **Tell a relevant story.** This makes your content more entertaining and more memorable. For example, share your most exasperated day of home educating in a homeschooling course.

- **Share a startling fact.** For example, if you're talking about a dangerous health issue, then state how many people die yearly from the disease. Sometimes getting people to take action that will help them can be facilitated by warning them about what might happen if they don't take action.

- **Get the audience to take part in a demo.** Ask them to actually try something out. For example, you might talk about the difficulty of patting one's stomach and rubbing circles on their head at the same time... and then transition to talking about how, likewise, multitasking is difficult.

- **Arouse curiosity.** E.G., "Later in this lesson, I'm going to share the biggest hack I've learned about setting up a home gym that can potentially save you thousands of dollars. I learned this the hard way, but you don't have to."

- **Ask questions.** E.G., "Have you let yourself get out of shape, and now even running short distances is hard?"

Next...

47. Inject Humor

If you can get people to crack a smile (or even laugh), then your viewers or readers will be hooked, and they'll stay engaged. Just be careful to know your audience, however, as your idea of humor may not fly with your particular customers.

TIP: Search for niche jokes or memes online. E.G., search for "dog jokes" if you've created an info product for dog owners.

Here's the next tip...

48. Share Fresh, New Tips

People love to learn new things about topics they are interested in. They feel GOOD when they see something they've never seen before, if it is related to solving a problem, reaching a goal, or better enjoying an interest. That's why you'll want to seek to share at least a few never-before-seen tips in your content, as people will associate the good feeling they get at seeing something new with you, your product, and your business.

49. Present Your Product In A Unique Way

Even if you're not exactly presenting new information to your viewers, you can certainly present it in a new way. For example, take a step-by-step process and create an acronym around it.

Here's an example: I once wrote a report entitled "How To Q.U.I.C.K.L.Y Create Content" where each of the 7 letters of "quickly" represented a different way to speed up content creation. ("Q" stood for "quotes"). There was likely nothing in these 7 methods that were unique to me, but the way I put the methods together was exclusively mine.

You can do the same.

50. Offer Examples

A good way to make your product more useful is to offer plenty of examples to help clarify what you're teaching. Just look at this report as an example of how to include plenty of examples.

This is one of the most important things you can do to add real value to your info products.

Examples make your points clearer. It allows your audience to better understand what you're teaching them because they can "see" it in a practical setting in your examples.

Seeing it in an example will help get them one step closer to seeing it in their own lives.

51. Two Tips For Being A Better Teacher

Not everyone is a natural-born teacher. But the good news is that you can learn how to be a more effective instructor. Check out these tips:

- **Beware of logical leaps.** If you're an expert in the field, then you're able to make logical leaps between two points. People with lesser experience may need more information. Fill in the gaps.

  For example, if you tell people to "get a domain name and hosting", then you're leaving out steps such as HOW to choose a good domain and how to change one's domain name servers. Know your audience so that you know how much detail to provide.

- **Provide examples, illustrations, videos, and similar aids.** Your students will understand the information better if they can see it in action.

  For example, if you're telling bodybuilders how to safely do a specific lift, then your content will be more useful if you provide a video or illustration of this lift.

Here's the next tip...

52. Help Non-Linear Thinkers

Not everyone thinks in a linear "A to B" fashion, especially when it comes to complex processes or concepts. That's why some people struggle to learn information solely from step-by-step information.

How do you help these thinkers?

Simple: create a mind map or process map to show the non-linear relations of all the steps and topics related to a process. You can create one quickly and easily using mind-mapping apps or software, like the one at MindJet.com.

53. Use Graphical Representations

If you're sharing data-heavy information, then it's a good idea to represent this data visually. That means sharing an infographic, chart, table, or similar item.

For example, if you're sharing data on the percentages of types of dogs who get a certain disease, you might share the data in a pie chart or table. That way, users can get the information they need at a glance.

54. Three Ways To Add Value To Your Product

If you can boost the perceived value of your product, then you'll have some very satisfied customers. Here are three ways to add value to your offer:

- **Provide tools.** E.g., worksheets, checklists, planners, templates, swipes, and similar.

- **Offer advanced information.** This information carries a higher perceived value than beginner-level information.

- **Include an attractive bonus package.** People should feel like the cost of the product is well worth the price they paid.

Which brings us to the next tip…

55. Create A High-Value Bonus Package

You can boost conversions plus boost the overall real and perceived value of your product by offering a bonus package.

On the following page you will find 15 examples of bonuses you can include in your package:

- Access to a private group or forum
- Another course on a related topic
- Related reports or eBooks
- Access to a membership site
- Multiple versions of the product (e.g., if you're offering a video course, then offer the audio and text transcripts as part of the bonus package)
- Apps/software/plugins
- Themes
- Templates
- Swipes
- Planners/calendars
- Checklists
- Worksheets
- Cheat sheets
- Mind maps/process maps
- Webinars

IDEA: What really adds value to your product offering is to include some level of coaching. Whether this is a one-time personal consultation, block of five email questions, group coaching (think pre-recorded video or webinar), or something similar, this really ups the value of your product offer.

Which brings us to the next tip...

56. How To Create A Successful Private Group

If you're offering access to a group as part of your product package, then the key to making this bonus valuable is to be sure you have an active group. Here's how to do that:

- **Send reminders to your students.** Use email, which shares the benefits of the group and encourages them to participate.

- **Post frequently to the group.** Reply to your students' questions, and start your own threads to encourage interaction.

- **Offer some of your best content in the group.** That way, people have a reason to keep coming back.

On a related note…

57. Three Ways To Engage Customers In Your Group

You want your students to engage in your group, which means you want them to ask and/or answer questions. Here are three ways to encourage more interaction:

- **Ask people what they think.** For example, post about an issue with two sides, and ask students for their opinion. Or simply ask an open-ended question.

- **Encourage people to share an experience.** For example, you might share your favorite marathon race and then ask readers to share theirs as well.

- **Showcase "posters of the month."** In other words, recognize and reward those who post often and/or offer thoughtful contributions.

Next…

58. Integrate Your Branding

As you develop your product, be sure to integrate your branding. Specifically:

- **Be sure your product reflects your branding, where appropriate.** For example, if your branding is about helping people take action and get results, then be sure you offer simple steps and provide tools with your product.

- **Include your branding within the product.** For example, the interior of a text-based product should include branding in the footer of the pages.

Bottom line: you want the look of your product to match your branding and solidify the way people feel about your brand.

59. A Secret For Creating A Great Product

Here's an unusual way to get a great end product: write your sales letter FIRST. This helps you get clear about the features and benefits you want your product to include. Then you can design your content around the promises you made in the sales letter.

In other words, your sales letter helps you nail down your big idea, solidify talking points for your product, and can even serve as a loose outline. Plus, the sales letter becomes a checklist for you to make certain all that you promise to your customers is delivered in your product as you create it.

60. Staying On Track

If you're creating the product yourself, then one of the biggest pitfalls is failing to complete the product on your own self-imposed deadline. Here's how to stay on track and be productive:

- **Create a specific plan.** This content-creation plan should include all the steps you need to take, along with a deadline for when you want to complete the product. Be sure to put this deadline on your calendar.

- **Make daily to-do lists.** Design this listing using "bite-size" chunks (small steps) so that you feel accomplished as you check items off your list every day. Be sure these lists reflect your overall goals and deadline. Having unrealistic expectations will often discourage and derail you, so keep the daily assignments reasonable and reachable.

- **Cut out distractions.** Turn off the TV, turn off your phone, and shut all windows on your computer except your word processor.

Now the next step...

3

Stage Three Details: Key Insights For Polishing Your Product, So That It Shines.

You've developed your product. Now it's time to look at the finishing touches, including polishing and distributing your product. Read on...

61. The #1 Bonus Mistake To Avoid

Most info publishers know they should include one or more bonuses with their products. But here's where many make a big mistake. Namely, they create a bonus package that backfires to the extent that it cheapens the entire product offering.

Here are the two main ways this happens:

1. **The bonus package is TOO big.** If you sell your product for $97 and then include a $997 bonus package, people are going to suspect that the product and the bonuses are over-priced / over-hyped and not really worth what you say they're worth.

2. **The bonus package is outdated/rehashed/not special.** This happens if you use older products or resell rights products for your bonuses. To make your package special, it's a good idea to create exclusive products for it that cannot be found anywhere else.

NOTE: Once more, let's return to the main purpose for creating an info product, which is to help your customers get an anticipated benefit. If you overload them with too much "stuff," they will get overwhelmed. If you include outdated/rehashed/not special materials, they either won't purchase or won't find it helpful. None of this helps them get to their goal. None of this satisfies the customer. None of this solidifies your credibility nor secures future business.

Bottom line...

Bonuses should add value, not detract from it.
Bonuses should aid in reaching a goal, not get in the way of it.

Next...

62. How To Price Your Product

How much should you charge for your product? Answer: do your research. Here are the steps:

1. Research similar products to find the range of selling prices in your niche.

2. Determine the strengths and weaknesses of these alternatives relative to your new product.

3. Check how your branding/positioning affects your price (where applicable).

4. Decide if your product is worth more or less than these other products.

5. Price your product based on the above steps.

6. Test your pricing to determine the sweet spot that produces the most profit.

HINT: It is better to compete on quality, not price. In other words, don't aim to offer the lowest-priced course in your niche; aim to offer the highest quality course in your niche.

Next...

63. Three Tips For Editing A Video-Based Product

To polish your video content and make it something special, follow these tips:

- **Retake rocky sections.** If there are a lot of ums and ahs, if the camera went out of focus, or if you stumbled on your words, then retake it, so your presentation is more professional.

- **Include appropriate background music.** But be sure it's at a low level so as not to drown out the narration.

- **Use transitions between segments.** This makes the video less "choppy" and keeps it visually interesting.

Next...

64. Three Tips For Editing A Text-Based Product

Here's where your average info product becomes fantastic. Follow these tips:

- **Read the product contents out loud.** This will show you where you need to smooth out a rocky section.

- **Tighten up the writing.** Edit out anything that's not absolutely necessary. No fluff, no filler.

- **Be sure the instructions are clear.** You may ask a friend to read your lessons and explain them back to you. If they can't do it, then you may need to provide more depth.

BIG KEY SECRET TO SUCCESS: It has been said that you never really understand something until you can explain it back in your own words. That's why the third tip above is so important. Eliminate any disconnects so your customers keep making progress. You don't want them to get stuck because they don't get what you're communicating to them.

Here's a related tip...

65. The #1 Proofing Tip

The best way to proof your content is to have someone else do it. That's because you're too close to your own work to see your mistakes. So, ask a trusted and knowledgeable friend to do it, or (better yet) hire a professional proofreader.

66. Polish Your Product

Before you launch your product to the world, you'll want to give it some spit and polish with these tips:

- **Be sure it's formatted for easy readability.** This means providing a lot of white space (no walls of text).

- **Insert graphics.** You can make your content more aesthetically pleasing by inserting infographics, photos, charts, tables, illustrations, and other relevant graphics.

- **Highlight important information.** You can do this with Johnson boxes, font colors, font sizing, bolding, italics, underlining, and similar. Be selective in what you highlight so that your product retains a professional image.

- **Check that all links work.** If you're promoting any affiliate products, run those links through a redirect on your own domain.

Next…

67. Check Your Facts

Don't even think about launching your product until you've checked and double-checked every statistic, claim, and other facts. Also, be sure you're getting your facts from reliable sources (such as scholarly articles, reputable news organizations, government sites, and similar).

> *SIDEBAR: If your reader finds incorrect information in your content, it will cause them to second-guess everything you say in the product. After all, they won't know when your content is reliable and when it is in error. If they can't trust it all, they can't trust any of it.*

68. Get Beta Readers

Beta readers will help ensure you have a high-quality, useful product. Check out these tips for choosing beta readers:

- **Be sure your beta readers are part of your target market.** If your ideal target is a woman in her 40s who's 20 pounds overweight and is looking to lose that weight, then your beta readers should be the same type of person.

- **Choose high-quality beta readers.** For example, choose people who regularly post on your social media pages or blog with insightful comments.

Next…

69. Test Your Titles

As you know, your title can make or break the success of your product. However, what looks like a good title to you may not actually be the highest-converting title. That's why you'll want to split-test titles to find the one that produces the most orders.

Key points:

- **Hold all variables constant.** When you test your titles, be sure that the title is the ONLY difference. Otherwise, you won't know what caused the change in conversion rate.

- **Use a split-testing tool.** Here's one for you to try: splittestmonkey.com.

Again, this will aid in the two big goals for your product: making a difference in the lives of other people and making money for your business. The higher your conversions, the more people who receive help from your product and the more orders you get from those people. Win win.

Here's the next tip...

70. Set Up An Autoresponder

You should automatically add everyone who buys your product into a follow-up autoresponder series. This series should be designed to:

- **Reduce buyer's remorse.** This, in turn, reduces refunds. (Good for you.)

- **Engage customers.** Encourage them to consume the content of your product and get results. (Good for them.)

- **Promote**. Offer additional products and services on the backend. (Good for you.)

- **Give additional free content.** Further aid them in reaching their goals. (Good for them.)

Be sure to use a trusted, reliable autoresponder such as AWeber.com, Keap.com, GetResponse.com, or similar.

71. 5 Things To Include In Your Customer Email

As you sit down to create your follow-up series, be sure to include these elements in the first email you send:

- **Thank the buyer.** They had plenty of other options from which to choose, so thank them for choosing your product. Ensure them that you are there to help.

- **Remind the buyer of billing details.** For example, let them know how the charges will appear on the credit card and if recurring charges will appear (and when).

- **Provide necessary links and instructions for download.** In other words, let buyers know how to get what they paid for. Do this even if your system immediately redirects them to the fulfillment page upon successful completion of their transaction.

- **Remind the buyer of the benefits of the offer.** Get them excited about the content of your product by telling them what they're about to learn. This builds anticipation and reduces buyer's remorse.

- **Encourage them to get started consuming the product.** If you have a big course, then it's a good idea to link them to a "Get Started Guide" or welcome letter to help them get going. Help them get a "quick win."

Here's a template you can use...

72. Template For An Effective First Email

Get customers excited about the product by using this template for the first email you send to them immediately after the sale:

Subject line: Thank you for choosing [Name of Product]!

Dear [First Name],

Thank you for choosing [name of product]. You are on your way to [getting some benefit] because [explain why this product is going to be helpful].

If you haven't already gained access to the product, you can do so now by [provide instructions and link].

I'm so excited that you're taking this course, and as soon as you start going through it, I know you'll be really excited and pleased too. That's because you'll discover:

[Insert a list of the top three to seven things the buyer will learn – you can even take these statements right from your sales letter.]

So, are you ready to start [getting some benefit]? Then open up [product name] and get started with Lesson 1, where you'll find out [main benefit/topic].

Thank you again for choosing [name of product]!

[sign off and your name]

P.S. If you have any questions at all, reach out to me by [provide contact information]. I'm here to help you in any way that I can. We're on this journey together!

73. Load Your Autoresponder

One of the most helpful, most profitable things you can do is load your autoresponder with a long-term series of follow-up email messages. These messages should…

- **Include a mix of content and promotions.** Some mailings should be strictly content, some mailings should be strictly promotions, and some mailings should be a blend of both.

- **Be queued for regular distribution intervals.** This is usually every 3-4 days, so you can keep in regular contact with your customers without being overly intrusive.

- **Further help the customer get desired outcomes.** Everything should work toward the same goal of your product, but offer "related, but different" avenues to do so.

Example: If your main product is related to losing weight by walking away the pounds, these additional mailings could focus on boosting metabolism, meal-planning, strength-training, motivation, and so forth. All of these work toward the goal of "losing weight" in ways that complement "walking away the pounds" without competing with it.

Next...

74. Get Customer Feedback

To improve your product further, you'll want to get feedback directly from your customers. Here are different ways to gather this feedback:

- **Request feedback via email.** You can start doing this about a week or two after a customer has purchased the product.

- **Gather feedback inside the membership site (where applicable).** You can put your request right on the landing page (what members see as soon as they log in).

- **Ask for feedback at the end of the product.** With this method, you can be assured that people actually viewed your content before they submitted feedback.

You can get more feedback by offering a bonus gift to anyone who sends you their thoughts on their purchase.

75. Use A Soft Sell

Sometimes you want to promote an offer in your product's content or in a follow-up email, but you don't want to insert a hard-sell ad. That's where the soft sell comes in, which is where you gently recommend a backend offer.

> *Let's suppose you're talking about how to set up an autoresponder. You might recommend a specific one by saying something like, "Be sure to go with a reputable autoresponder. I trust AWeber for all my lists – check them out at…"*

See how that works? You're pointing your customer to something they are going to need anyway, providing a shortcut by sharing who you trust and use yourself (so they don't have to spend time researching), and earning a commission for the referral by using an affiliate link.

76. Splinter Your Info Product

If you have created a multi-module or multi-lesson info product, then you have a few other strategies to consider taking advantage of, because you can also 'splinter off' one of the best modules and offer that to your prospects either as a free offer (AKA "Lead Magnet") or a low-cost frontend offer (AKA "Tripwire Product"). Anyone who sees the individual lesson is sure to want to purchase the entire product, which makes it easy to sell the full product offering on the backend.

77. Exude Professionalism

As you're preparing your product for sale, you'll want to make sure that your product looks professional at every point.

This includes:

- Professional interior layout (for text products) or video production (for videos)

- Quality cover graphics

- Polished web design and content

- Well-written content

- Accurate description of your product in the sales process

- Professional customer service

- Well-crafted follow-up emails

- Trustworthy business practices

Together, this makes a great impression, boosts conversions, and boosts customer satisfaction.

78. Outsource The Sales Letter

Your sales letter can make or break the success of your product. As such, this is definitely one thing you'll want to outsource if you don't have the copywriting skills to do it yourself.

Look for copywriters on Google, ask for recommendations from friends, and/or post projects on freelancing sites like upwork.com. In all cases, do your due diligence so that you end up with a professional who knows how to generate high conversion rates without damaging your reputation.

Make sure your copywriter (or you) goes by this best practice for your sales letter:

Give prospects hope, not hype.

That is, communicate how it is that what you're teaching in the product can give the prospect the help they want and need without making outlandish claims and empty promises that "sound good" but don't deliver.

You want to give your prospects real hope, not false hope.

79. DOs And DON'TS For Convincing Prospects To Become Buyers

When persuading people to buy your product it should not be about trying to manipulate them to buy something they don't really need, but instead about helping them see your info product as something they do need to reach their goal.

Here are some DOs and DON'Ts for this…

- DON'T manipulate people into making a buying decision by preying on their emotions and playing mind-games about their fears.

- DO let them know that you understand what it's like to be where they are and that you can help them get to where they want to be.

- DON'T try to make people feel like they aren't serious about reaching their goal or are foolish if they don't buy your product.

- DO explain why buying your product is a wise decision for them in trying to reach their goal because it really does deliver.

- DON'T ignore their objections ("I can't afford it," "I can't do it," etc.) as unimportant or illegitimate concerns.

- DO address their objections by letting them know how you and your product can help them overcome their legitimate concerns.

- DON'T attempt to force them to buy something they don't really need at this point by using the "fear of missing out."

- DO help them see why buying and implementing your training right away will help them reach their goal more quickly (if it will).

- DON'T give them reasons to say "no" to your product offer because they are concerned it won't work for them and will be a waste of money.

- DO give them reasons to say "yes" to your product offer by providing proof of your claims (using photo evidence, videos, testimonials, and case studies) as well as a strong money-back guarantee.

Next…

80. Sell Your Videos Here

If you've created a video-based info product, then one place you'll want to consider selling it is on Udemy.com. That's because this platform helps you market video courses, so it can be an additional hands-free way to make money. Just be sure you read and follow all guidelines before submitting your video-based product to this platform.

81. Setting Up Your Own Platform

If you want to make the most money with your product, then sell it on your own platform (rather than a third-party platform that takes a cut of the profits). If you're selling a multipart course, then you may use one of these three options:

- **Use an autoresponder.** If you're simply delivering modules and you don't need bells and whistles, then you can use an autoresponder (like Aweber) to deliver each installment of the product.

- **Set up a membership site script.** This is a good option if you need features like a member forum, pages where people can download the information, and drip-fed content. Here's one example: Membergate.com

- **Use a WordPress plugin.** If your site is set up on a WordPress platform, then you might use a membership plugin such as the one found at S2Member.com

Next...

82. Determining Delivery Details

If you're drip feeding multipart content, here's a question: *When will you deliver the modules? Daily? Weekly? Monthly? Some other schedule?*

Ask yourself these questions:

- How long will it take the average customer to consume a module?

- How long will it take the average customer to implement the information learned in a module?

- How long will it take for the average customer to complete the overall process or reach their goal?

- How many modules do you have?

    For example, if you're publishing a weight loss product and you expect customers to take about three months to reach their goals, then you might share one module per week for three months.

NOTE: Unless you have a good reason to do so, you will generally want to give customers access to the entire product at the time of the purchase, so they work through it at their own individual pace. Some exceptions include: When the customer is making multiple payments or the information is so comprehensive, it would be a deterrent to progress to view it all at once.

83. A Helpful Idea For Reducing Refunds

This is very simple but very effective: offer ongoing bonuses to those who remain customers. To reduce refunds, be sure that some of your BEST bonuses are delivered after the refund period has expired. Your customers will stick around just to get their hands on these valuable gifts.

84. Boosting Your Product's Credibility

Here's a simple way to build credibility: get an endorsement, testimonial, or even a foreword created by an expert. Alternatively, you might get one or more bonus materials created by other well-known experts in your niche.

85. The #1 High-Value Bonus Your Customers Will Love

Here's a great bonus to add to your package: either personal or group coaching.

Here are the advantages:

- Coaching carries a high value, so it boosts the value of your entire package.

- This bonus helps students take action and get good results, which translates to higher customer satisfaction and customers who become repeat buyers.

- You can offer limited coaching as a bonus, with the option for students to buy more coaching on the backend.

Next...

86. Assigning Homework

One good way to engage people, get them to take action, and boost their satisfaction with your information is to assign "homework" at the end of each lesson. Even better is if students send their homework to you to receive feedback.

For example, students in a copywriting course can send three headlines to you to critique.

Assignments are a "must-include" for every course as it ensures that the customer knows what the next practical step in their progress toward the goal is and encourages them to take it.

87. Create A Quick Start Guide

This is particularly useful if you have a large or in-depth information product – perhaps housed inside a membership site – as you can give people an overview of what they need to do to get started. You might even offer a checklist of the steps they need to take (with detailed instructions for each step inside the main content itself).

TIP: The more things you build into your product's content to help your customers get "quick wins" by taking steps and making real progress, the better.

88. Write A "Stick" Letter

A "stick" letter is designed to reduce buyer's remorse and get people engaged and using the content. Your welcome email in the initial customer follow-up email is similar to the stick letter. The difference is that the stick letter appears inside the membership site (where applicable) or inside the product itself. You may even use the same letter for your welcome email and stick letter. Posting it in two places (the initial email and inside the product or site) ensures people will see it.

89. Offer Unannounced Bonuses

You can offer these bonuses right on the initial download page, as well as a week or two after customers have purchased the product. Offering unannounced bonuses is a good way to boost customer satisfaction.

NOTE: One of the foundational guidelines for business is this: under-promise and over-deliver. Providing these unannounced bonuses is a great way to keep adding more value to the initial purchase.

90. Gather Testimonials

The idea here is to solicit testimonials from your satisfied customers that you can then use in your marketing materials. Here are three ways to gather these testimonials:

- **Ask for testimonials in your follow-up emails.** Let customers know they'll be doing you a big favor if they submit their testimonials to you.

- **Make a testimonial request at the end of the product.** Be sure to include a contact link or email alongside your call to action.

- **Solicit testimonials directly.** For example, if you provide personal coaching as a bonus, then at the end of the session, you can ask the student to provide a testimonial.

Testimonials help prospects become paying customers because they see other people who have used your product and are happy that they did.

Here's a related tip...

91. Collect Together Case Studies

Your customers want to believe your claims, but they've been burned before. That's why you need to prove your claims, and one good way to do this is through case studies.

Here's the key: your case study needs to provide lots of data and evidence.

For example, if you're doing a case study with a weight loss product, then the data should include before and after weights and measurements, as well as plenty of pics and/or videos.

That's what a case study does, showcases the progress from "before" to "after." It helps others "see" what it looked like for someone who came to you for help and the kind of help your product actually delivered.

You can then send these case studies to prospects via email, post them on your blog, include them in your sales materials, or even post on social media.

92. Start Planning Spin-Off Products

Anyone who purchases your product is likely to purchase something else from you. That's why you'll want to create other closely related products to sell to this same audience.

For example:

- If you're selling a product on bodybuilding, then you can also sell a more specific product on competition bodybuilding.

- If you're selling a product on social media marketing, you might sell a targeted product that focuses on how to create successful Facebook campaigns.

- If you're selling a product on organic gardening, you might sell another product that's all about identifying, preventing, and getting rid of garden pests.

Next...

93. 11 Places To Cross-Promote Your Product

One good place to promote your product is internally, meaning within your sales funnel and on your platforms. Here are 11 places to do it:

- Promote within your Lead Magnet
- Mention it on your subscription thank you pages
- Sell it on your paid product download pages
- Cross-promote it from within your other paid products
- Upsell it on an order form
- Sell it inside your prospect emails
- Promote it to your customer mailing lists
- Blog about it
- Tell your social media followers about it
- Share it to your private groups/forums
- Mention it to your webinar attendees

Here's another tip...

94. Check The Product Orientation

Here's a simple tip: if you want to engage your readers, then be sure your product's content focuses on them and their problems.

- Use words like "you" more than "I" or "me." This focuses the content on your readers/viewers.

- Keep personal stories and autobiographies succinct. You can get personal to build relationships, show you understand the problem, establish your credentials and create more memorable content. But once the story is done, pivot back to focusing on the reader.

Here's the next idea...

95. 4 Ways To Accelerate Product Creation

One way to speed up product creation is to pick the format which is fastest for you to create (text or video). But you shouldn't choose your format based on creation speed; rather you should choose it based on what best fits the content. That's why you'll want to check out these other ideas for accelerating product creation:

- **Outsource**. Just be sure to do your due diligence so that you have a good experience.

- **Start with private label rights content.** If you choose high-quality PLR (like the type you find at LicensingClub.com), then you may only need to tweak it slightly to create your product.

- **Repurpose existing content.** Do you already have content on hand that you could turn into a new product? Then start with that to make content creation faster.

- **Use technology**. If you're typing content, then speech-to-text software such as Dragon Naturally Speaking or one of many smartphone apps can speed up content creation.

Next...

96. Three Content Creation Mistakes To Avoid

To save yourself time, money, and heartache down the road, check out these three content-creation mistakes to avoid:

- **Confusing yourself with the customer.** Sometimes info publishers make mistakes because they personally wouldn't want something or to do something. But you are not your customer. For example, just because you may not personally use PLR materials doesn't mean your customers won't gladly use them.

- **Asking the wrong question.** Sometimes product creators ask themselves, "What do I know that I can create a product around?" However, the first question you should ask yourself is this: "What do my students want to know?" (You can compare the answers to the latter alongside what you know in order to pick a good topic to teach.)

- **Creating just one course or product.** The vast majority of product creators won't build a successful business with just one product. That's why you need to create an entire sales funnel full of products, as many times the profits in your business will come from the backend.

Next…

97. Three Questions To Ask Before You Launch Your Product

Before you launch your final product, ask yourself these three questions:

- Does each lesson achieve your goal for learner outcomes?

- Have you provided enough information in each lesson for users to solve their problems, reach their goals, or better enjoy their interests?

- Is there anything else you can add to your product to make it even better/more useful?

Once you feel good about the answers to those questions, then you're ready to put the finishing touches to it and release it.

98. Planning Your Sales Funnel

As you're planning your product, you should also be planning the sales funnel around it. Specifically, ask yourself these questions:

- What sort of free content and products (AKA Lead Magnets) will you use to introduce people into your sales funnel?

- What front-end products (AKA Tripwire Offers) will you use to help prospects become paying customers?

    TIP: You can splinter off a module/lesson from your main product to use as a front-end product.

- How will you follow up with your front-end buyers to further help them through a purchase of your foundational offer (your main product offering)?

- What products will you sell on the backend (your flagship product offers) to your front-end product buyers?

This is, of course, how you create maximum profit for your business. And that's what's in it for you. But it's also how you create a maximum difference in the lives of other people. That's what's in it for them. As they progress from prospect to paying customer to repeat customer, they should also be progressing in reaching and exceeding their goals.

A sales funnel is not just about sales for you.
It's also about satisfaction for your customers.

Next...

99. Four Characteristics Every Free Offer Ought To Possess

A free offer (AKA Lead Magnet) is an important part of your sales process because it's what introduces people to your sales funnel.

In other words, it's what connects you and your prospects for the first time, establishes your relationship, and helps them to start "knowing, liking, and trusting" you as someone who can help them.

It could be any number of products, from one of your lesson modules to any other type of related eBook, video, webinar, app, tools, or other resources. Be sure your free offer / Lead Magnet possesses these characteristics:

- It's highly related to your main product. In fact, it should naturally lead to your front-end/tripwire offer (and/or the product).

- It's in-demand. Do your market research to find out what your audience wants.

- It's valuable. You should be able to easily sell it for $25, $50, or more by itself, even though you're giving it away for free.

- It's high quality. It should make a great impression on your prospects.

Next...

100. Check, Check, Double-Check

Before you release your product, do one last check to be sure everything is right.

This includes checking:

- All links in the product work
- All links on the sales page/website work
- The payment process works as intended
- The autoresponder works as intended
- All links within the emails work
- Everything is proofed and polished (product, sales letter, and autoresponder emails)

Now the final step...

101. Testing Your Sales Process

Once you release your product, then it's time to optimize everything by testing your sales process and other factors. Here are the top factors you can test:

- The name of your product
- The price
- The offer as a whole (e.g., the bonus package and how you position the product in the market)
- The web design
- The headline
- The call to action
- The format (video sales letter vs. text sales letter)
- The postscript of your sales letter
- The eCover graphics

You can also test the other parts of your sales process, such as the free offer / Lead Magnet type and title, the lead page sales copy, the subject lines on the follow-up emails, the calls to action in the follow-up emails, and similar.

You can use a tool like SplitTestMonkey.com or Piwik.org, plus you can use built-in testing tools (like those in your email autoresponder service).

Now let's wrap things up...

Conclusion

You just discovered 101 tips, insights, ideas, suggestions, methods, hacks, templates, shortcuts, resources, and lists for mastering the art of information product creation. You can use these tips to polish and improve an existing product or perhaps use them to help you create your first product successfully. Either way, the key is to put this information to work for you as soon as possible.

While I've given you a lot of information and ideas here in this handy guide, if you're keen to receive some more help, guidance, and personal support with your Info Publishing business moving forward, then read on through these final few paragraphs because you are going to be pleasantly surprised with an exciting update I have for you with regards to the ***Serious About Six Figures A Year*** online training program.

Originally, I created the ***Serious about Six Figures A Year*** program to compliment my ***Six Figures A Year In Info Publishing*** book. The course was originally 4-months long and included 4 deep-dive training sessions into the 4 key areas of success that I wrote about in the book.

However, in recent months, the course has been completely re-written and extended and now centers around 6 different areas of running a successful and profitable information publishing business. We call these areas *The Successful Six*, and they are:

- How To Produce Orders
- How To Build Your List
- How To Generate Traffic
- How To Grow Your Income
- How To Create Content
- How To Work Less Hours

I'm especially excited to be able to share these extra strategies and insights with you because once you're able to control and manage these areas of your business confidently, you're going to experience a huge uplift in your business growth, your profits, and ultimately the way you enjoy life.

If you would like to discover further details of the new **Serious About Six Figures A Year** home study course, then you are invited to go to the following page, which is just for you as a loyal customer and reader of this book.

www.SeriousAboutSixFigures.com/101

I highly recommend you take this important step in your entrepreneurial journey and discover all the benefits that membership has to offer.

Finally, I sincerely hope that you have enjoyed reading *The Handy Book Of Great Ideas For Information Publishers,* and you have noted and committed yourself to implementing multiple ideas that you have discovered from reading this book.

Here's to your continued success.

Recommended Resources

Six Figures A Year. Our best-selling book that shows you the four keys to success for setting up a simple $100k+ a year business from the comfort of your own home. Get your copy for free at:

www.SixFiguresAYear.com

Serious About Six Figures. An extended training program which follows on from the 'Six Figures A Year' book, which shows you how to produce orders, build your list, generate traffic, grow your income, create content and work less hours while still banking $100k+ a year.

www.*SeriousAboutSixFigures.com*

Product Licensing Formula. Licensing can also save you hundreds of hours and/or thousands of dollars compared to creating content from scratch yourself or hiring a freelance ghost-writer to create content for you. Discover how to use the power of licensing instead. Until now relatively little information has been made available about how to do this, but all that is about to change.

www.ProductLicensingFormula.com

The Internet Marketing Newsletter (monthly PLR). If you are an author, speaker, coach, consultant who (like us) teaches online or digital marketing to your clients, then your biggest headache has just been solved. Instead of struggling to research and write new content each month. You can now license our award-winning newsletter. Join today and each month you will receive the full PLR rights to a full 32 page professionally designed newsletter which you can rebrand, publish and profit from.

www.TheInternetMarketingNewsletter.com/plr

Recommended Resources

Unfair Advantage Cheat Sheets. Over 880 pages of fill-in-the-blanks templates, swipe files, case studies, training tutorials and more to make writing anything faster, easier, and better. An essential resource for every content author and business owner.
www.UnfairAdvantageCheatSheets.com

WP Download Page Protector. A software solution for WordPress which protects your product download pages. It's a fact that some people will avoid paying for your products if they can. This happens both offline and online. Now you can quickly and easily protect your product from being stolen when you back is turned and ensure only paying customers can access your download pages.
www.WPDownloadPageProtector.com

WP Affiliate Surge. A software solution for WordPress which enables you to quickly and easily create a fully loaded promotional tools page that will attract affiliates and help them to promote your next product launch.
www.WPAffiliateSurge.com

Rebrandio. A software solution for WordPress which enables you to quickly and easily create an unlimited number of viral, re-brandable PDF reports, which when past around via social media and email could start an avalanche of free traffic to your website, that you couldn't stop (*even if you wanted to*).
www.Rebrand.io